The Sea Route
to Asia

EXPLORATION AND DISCOVERY

The Conquest of Mexico

The Early French Explorers of North America

Exploration of the California Coast

The Exploration of the Moon

The English Colonization of America

The European Rediscovery of America

Explorers of the American West

Explorers of the South Pacific

The First Voyage Around the World

The Journey of Lewis and Clark

Pathfinders of the American Frontier

The Sea Route to Asia

The Spanish Exploration of Florida

The Spanish Exploration of South America

The Spanish Exploration of the Southwest

The Sea Route to Asia

The adventures of the Portuguese explorers,
from Prince Henry the Navigator to
Bartholomeu Dias and Vasco da Gama

David Rutsala

Mason Crest Publishers
Philadelphia

Mason Crest Publishers
370 Reed Road
Broomall PA 19008

Mason Crest Publishers' world wide web address is
www.masoncrest.com

First printing

1 3 5 7 9 8 6 4 2

Library of Congress Cataloging-in-Publication Data
on file at the Library of Congress

ISBN 1-59084-046-1

EXPLORATION AND DISCOVERY

Contents

1 Lost at Sea 7
2 The Navigator's Vision 13
3 The First Expeditions 21
4 In the Wake of the Navigator 29
5 Gama Sails for India 39
6 The Portuguese Empire 47

Chronology 58
Glossary 60
Further Reading 62
Internet Resources 62
Index 63

Portuguese ships sail through choppy waters around the Cape of Good Hope, near the southernmost tip of Africa. In 1487, a Portuguese captain named Bartholomeu Dias attempted to become the first European to sail around Africa and reach the Indian Ocean.

Lost at Sea

COMMANDER BARTHOLOMEU Dias looked out on a calm and tranquil sea. After the 13-day storm that had rocked his fleet, he should have welcomed this sight: dead calm as far as the eye could see. But he did not.

His supplies were running low. His crew was frightened. There was no land in sight. And he was lost. This was a combination destined to frighten even the most experienced *mariner*. Dias needed to swallow his fear, however, and make a decision.

The fleet he commanded had been ordered to round the southern tip of Africa, thereby opening a sea route to Asia. This was a feat that no sailor had yet achieved. If Dias was successful, his king and country would have access to the riches of India and the East. The expedition would make or break Dias's career. He could not fail—he must not fail!

When the storm hit, the fleet had been at sea for almost six months. The storm had pushed them south of their last known position, but how far south? Dias did not know, and he had no way of finding out. Like all the sailors of his day, he had no effective means of determining *longitude*.

Longitude is one's relative position north or south on the earth. It is expressed through a set of imaginary lines drawn on maps and globes. A reliable means for determining longitude on the open seas was not created until the mid-18th century, nearly 300 years after Dias' expedition.

Dias made an educated guess and ordered the fleet east. It was a good guess. Unless the storm had pushed them past the southern tip of Africa, an idea Dias could not even remotely entertain on that first calm day, the coast must lie east.

A day passed. The sea remained calm, and there was no sign of land.

The crew was afraid. They had given themselves up for dead during the storm, and now they faced an even more frightening prospect: death by starvation on the open seas. This idea was made vividly real by the smell of rotting meat—their food supply—rising from the hold.

As the sun set on that first day, Dias remained confident about his guess and held his fleet to the course. He was confident that Africa lay to the east—it had to. As the second day dawned, however, doubt must have crept into his mind. Could they have sailed past the southern tip of Africa? Had the storm managed a feat no explorer could?

The 1487 voyage of Bartholomeu Dias was intended to complete nearly 60 years of exploration by the Portuguese. Since the early part of the 15th century, sailors from Portugal had been seeking a sea route to Asia by following the unknown coastline of Africa.

If he ordered the fleet north, he could find out. This was a decision that could cause problems, however. If he was wrong, it would send the fleet in the wrong direction—not toward the African coast, but in the direction the ships had come from. In other words, they would be sailing back toward Europe. If he made this decision, he could not be wrong.

The crew must have pressured him to sail north. This was the farthest south any of them had ever been. These were seas they had never seen, skies they had never dreamed about. Everything they knew lay north. Every moment in their lives, from their births to this very moment, lay north.

All through that second day, these pressures must have weighed heavily on Dias's mind. One can imagine arguments with his pilots and the frightened crew. One can imagine him drawing on his years of experience, seeking the right decision, the smart decision. But what was the right decision? And how could he decide? All during this day, he must have watched the sea as the fleet continued to sail east.

Hour after hour passed, and still there was no land in sight. Luckily, the seas remained calm. This fact, however, might have merely increased Dias's sense of solitude and fear. Finally, late on that second day, he made a decision, ordering the fleet north. This was the most important decision Dias had ever made. But was it the right decision?

A ship's size is often measured in tons. This does not mean the ship's actual weight; instead, it indicates the weight of water displaced by the ship. The ships commanded by Bartholomeu Dias were each about 50 tons—the largest Portuguese ships of the time. In 1492, Christopher Columbus's *Santa Maria* was about 100 tons. The *Mayflower*, which brought the Pilgrims to America in 1620, was 106 tons. By comparison, the ocean liner *Titanic* was 66,000 tons—1,320 times larger than Dias's 50-ton ships.

History does not tell us why he made this decision. Maybe he bowed to pressure from the crew, as he would later in the mission. Maybe he truly believed he had rounded the southern tip of Africa. Or maybe he was just performing a common "L" maneuver, used for centuries by lost sailors.

Whatever caused Dias to turn his ships north, we can be certain he knew the risks. The next several hours would decide the success or failure of his mission. Would Dias become the hero of his age? Would he marked as a failure, even a coward? Or would Dias become just another casualty in the great story of Portuguese exploration?

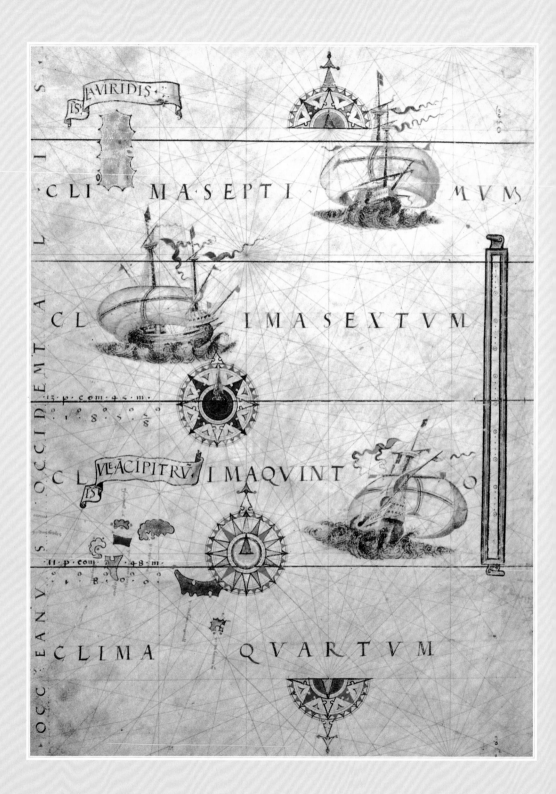

This is a detail from a 15th century Portuguese map. The lines on the map that radiate from central points were used by sailors to navigate from port to port. The small ships drawn on this map are caravels, a sturdy vessel developed by the Portuguese to use as they explored the coast of Africa.

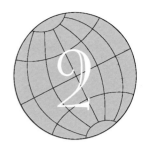

The Navigator's Vision

A CENTURY before Bartholomeu Dias set out on his important voyage, the idea of Portugal leading the greatest program of exploration the world had ever known seemed remote. The country did possess unique geographic characteristics. The western coast faced the largely unexplored and unfathomable Atlantic Ocean, and only a tiny *strait* separated Portugal from the equally mysterious continent of Africa. The country also possessed many *navigable* waterways, and a large percentage of its population worked on the water in the fishing and shipping trades.

These factors alone might have produced some explorers. Portugal's contribution to the age of exploration, however, looms far larger than a few lone explorers and owes every-thing to the efforts of one man. In his day, he was known as Prince Henry, or Enriques Infante, but history would dub him "Prince Henry the Navigator."

He never went on a mission of exploration himself, but Prince Henry the Navigator created a program of explo-ration unlike any the world had ever seen. This was an orga-nized, national endeavor that lasted well past his death and led to the *circumnavigation* of Africa and the discovery of Portugal's sea route to Asia. It also led to important advances in ship building and the *maritime* sciences.

More than 700 years before Henry was born, a new reli-gion called Islam had developed in the Middle East. The new beliefs soon spread throughout northern Africa and even into Europe, where most of the people were Christian. Around 750 A.D., Portugal and Spain were overrun by the Moors, a tribe of *Muslims* from north Africa. The Christians and Muslims hated each other, so brutal fighting continued for centuries.

By the time Prince Henry was 16, the Moors had been forced out of Portugal. However, the fighting continued. His father, King John I, decided to attack one of the Moors' strongholds—the city of Ceuta. This important port was located on the coast of North Africa. For several years, Prince Henry helped to plan the Portuguese attack. He put

Prince Henry the Navigator

Prince Henry was born in 1394, the third son of King John I. In his youth, Prince Henry dreamed of winning great military vic-tories. In 1414, he finally got his chance. Henry and his brothers played a vital role in the capture of Ceuta, a Muslim port in north Africa.

For Henry, the capture of Ceuta did not whet his appetite for further military action. Instead, it opened the young prince's mind to the possibility of exploring Africa. He saw his soldiers bringing back riches from the defeated city—riches that had arrived in the city by way of the African caravan trade. He began collecting information about this rich and mysterious continent.

Henry would not win great military victories, but he might do the next best thing. He might be able to bring his country vast wealth. This dream, spurred on by stories of the crusades, led to the creation of the great era of Portuguese exploration.

together a 200-ship fleet. When this *armada* launched in August 1414, they surprised the Muslims and captured Ceuta in a day.

As the third son of King John I, it was unlikely that Prince Henry would ever become king of Portugal. His older brother Duarte was next in line for the throne. If something happened to Duarte, the second brother, Pedro, would rule until Duarte's son was old enough to become king.

The great success of the Portuguese sea attack made Prince Henry interested in the idea of sea exploration. He believed that through exploration, Portugal could establish trade relations with other countries, determine the strength of their enemies, seek allies in the fight against the Muslims, and spread the message of Christianity.

Henry understood the political power of these arguments, but he also knew they might be difficult to sell to the public. So he backed up his arguments with popular ideas. For example, he stressed as a goal the search for Prester John. Prester John was a mythical Christian ruler who was said to possess a kingdom somewhere in Asia. Prester John did not exist, but many in Henry's time fervently believed that he did. Henry does not seem to have been one of the believers, but he knew the power of the story, so he used it.

Prince Henry ruled out the possibility of exploring Africa by land. The Muslims controlled the safest routes, and the Prince's advisors deemed all other routes too dangerous. This left only one alternative: sea exploration.

Sea exploration, however, was still new, and Portugal had neither the means nor the methods for exploring the open seas. In order to achieve his dreams, Henry would need to completely revitalize the industries and sciences of his age. He did just that.

Henry created a revolutionary way of looking at the problem of exploration. He saw the process clearly: exploration was both a scientific and political endeavor. So he organized the process into a set of different problems and employed top people from all over the known world to solve these problems.

First, he attacked the problem of the maps. During the 15th century, most maps were little more than cartoons— rough, fanciful documents that served almost no navigational function. Prince Henry changed all this. He required his sailors to keep accurate records of their voyages and employed experienced *cartographers* to use these new findings to create more accurate maps of the explored regions. The accuracy of these maps made sailors less afraid to venture far from the waters they knew, and changed European ideas about the world.

Next, Prince Henry gathered information about the latest and most effective navigating instruments. He made

In the fifteenth century, many saw the compass as an instrument with magical powers.

Tools such as the cross-staff, shown in this 1584 illustration, were used to determine a ship's position. The navigator lined up the horizon with the sun, then checked a mathematical table to determine the ship's latitude.

more effective compasses. Rather than using more complicated instruments for determining **latitude** (such as the **astrolabe**), he gave his sailors a **cross-staff**. This was a simple instrument that sailors could use to measure the position of the sun relative to the horizon. With the cross-staff, sailors had a better idea of where they were at sea.

Next, Henry revolutionized the field of ship building. Combining the best elements of Arab, Tunisian, Egyptian, and Greek design, the Prince's shipbuilders created a ship called the **caravel**. It was small, broad, and low, with a fixed rudder. The caravel had both square sails, as other European ships did, and triangular sails called lateens used by Arab ships to help them maneuver. These rugged ships possessed the strength and mobility required for exploration.

Beginning in 1419, Henry organized all these programs from a centralized location. He did not work in the nation's capital, Lisbon. Instead, Henry established his headquarters

This model represents the typical Portuguese caravel of the 15th century, as developed by Prince Henry the Navigator. The triangular sails pictured here were called lateen sails; they helped the ship turn and maneuver. Prince Henry probably adopted this rigging from Arab ships that sailed in the Mediterranean. Caravels were often rigged with square sails as well; these would allow more speed in a following wind.

in Sagres, a city on the extreme southern tip of Portugal. This decision moved Henry away from political dealings at the capital and closer to the sea.

Prince Henry the Navigator certainly had a great vision, but would he be able to achieve his goals? And would the public and the court of Portugal wait as he poured huge sums of money into this great endeavor?

As Portuguese sailors explored the coast of Africa, others followed to exploit the continent's riches. The Portuguese developed a network of trading posts along the coast. This fort, located at Cape Verde, is a popular tourist spot today.

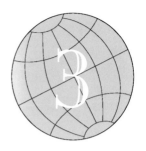

The First Expeditions

PRINCE Henry's first expeditions did not succeed. The sailors he sent did not make great discoveries or bring back valuable information. It seemed that Henry's program of exploration might fail before it really began.

Then, in 1432, he had his first important success. An expedition searching for land in the open Atlantic discovered the Azore Islands. Soon, Portuguese settlers had established colonies on these islands. Prince Henry gained great fame for adding these new lands to Portugal's rule. The success of this mission helped the prince continue his program of exploration. The next goal would be passing Cape Bojador, on the west coast of Africa.

> **Prince Henry himself never sailed on missions of exploration. He always sent other captains, while he organized the trips from Sagres.**

Cape Bojador presented many dangers to mariners of the 15th century. Strong currents and heavy *surges* lined the coast, and schools of fish created strange whirlpools. These dangers were only part of the problem, however. Portuguese pilots had faced similar conditions elsewhere and had successfully conquered them. The real barrier had nothing to do with the sea. The real barrier was fear. Arabs had dubbed the sea beyond Cape Bojador "the Sea of Darkness," and legends claimed the end of the world lay beyond this point. Other stories spoke of sea monsters and gelatinous seas that would prevent ships from moving.

However, Prince Henry did not believe these stories. Cape Bojador could be rounded, and Portuguese sailors were going to do it.

By 1433, 15 expeditions had attempted this feat. All had failed. When a captain named Gil Eannes returned from his first attempt, he told the Prince that Cape Bojador was impassable. Henry would not accept this. In 1434, he ordered Eannes to try again.

When Eannes reached the cape, he sailed west, deciding he would rather face the open seas than the dangers of Cape

Bojador. When he finally turned south again, the cape was already behind him. He landed on the coast of Africa, finding a barren beach with few signs of life—not inviting terrain to say the least, but hardly the "end of the world." With this expedition, Eannes had achieved more than merely rounding the cape—he removed the barrier of fear that had hampered further exploration. Now the real era of Portuguese exploration could begin.

In 1435, Eannes set out again, accompanied this time by a Portuguese nobleman named Alphonso Baldaya. This expedition extended the African coastline known to the Portuguese another 50 *leagues* (about 150 miles) down the African coast. Eannes and Baldaya also brought back the first reports of human settlements below Cape Bojador.

The barrier of the cape now behind him, Prince Henry set

A league is a unit of distance that is equal to about three miles.

new goals: the search for rivers or other waterways that the Portuguese could use to sail into the interior of Africa, and the capture of African natives who could be sold as slaves. This sent a message that his expeditions could make Portugal a rich and powerful nation. Henry knew that he would need to start seeing results from his vast program of exploration, or the court would not support his efforts.

Baldaya's second expedition in 1436 failed to capture

any natives as slaves. He did claim, however, to have found a water route in the African interior. In fact, Baldaya failed on both counts. He brought back no slaves, and what he assumed to be a river turned out to be a large *inlet*.

In 1444, Eannes ventured out again. This time, he brought back over 200 Africans, who could be sold as slaves. The capture of African natives altered public opinion in Portugal. Henry's expeditions were no longer viewed as a waste of time and money.

During the next several years, Portuguese captains such as Eannes, Antão Gonçalves, Nuno Tristão, Alvise

A negative legacy of Portuguese exploration was the capture and sale of Africans as slaves. The practice began in the 1440s as a way to help fund continued voyages of discovery. Within a century blacks were being sold to Spanish colonies in the Caribbean and Portugal's colonies in Brazil and in the east.

Cadamosto, and Diogo Gomes made many voyages down the coast of Africa. They carefully mapped the coastlines they followed. In 1446, Portuguese captains reached Cape Verde. This expedition found that vegetation along the African coast increased in density the farther south they went. The discovery of lush lands beneath the equator caused a sensation. It forced many people to rethink their ideas about Africa, if not the whole world. Africa was not a land of deserts. Rather, to the south it had an abundance of wildlife, plants, and people.

While sailing around the cape, the Portuguese landed on the Cape Verde Islands, off the west coast of Africa. They also charted the Senegal and Gambia rivers on the mainland. However, these rivers did not lead to the interior of the continent. It would be more than 10 years before an expedition would attempt to map either of these waterways.

Despite the scientific importance of these discoveries and the beginning of the slave trade, the expeditions were still not making enough money. By 1450, Prince Henry was deeply in debt, and tensions arose with Castile—a kingdom on the Iberian peninsula that is now part of Spain—over claims on African lands. The dispute was finally settled in Portugal's favor, but only after intervention by Pope Nicholas V. Henry desperately needed another success.

Henry used the popular myth of Prester John again to

Prince Henry used the myth of Prester John, a powerful Christian king who people believed would help the Portuguese defeat the Muslims, as a motivation for exploration. This detail from a 16th-century map of the east coast of Africa shows the legendary king seated in the area where his kingdom was thought to exist.

get it. In 1456 he ordered an expedition up the Gambia, claiming the sailors would find Abyssinia and its fabled Christian ruler, Prester John. A mission did sail up the Gambia, but of course neither the mythical ruler nor his kingdom was found.

Henry, a masterful politician, turned this uneventful expedition to his favor. He claimed the expedition had come within a hairsbreadth of reaching Abyssinia, only to be turned back by violent natives

During his trip up the Gambia River, Diogo Gomes met African natives and traded beads and cloth for 180 pounds of gold.

with poison arrows. The commander of the mission, Diogo Gomes, backed up Henry's account. He gave details about priest-kings under Prester John who ruled in the area. The commander may have believed some of this, but he cannot have sailed too far up the Gambia. The Barracunda Rapids lie only 200 miles inland, making the river impassable.

Portuguese scholars and the public, however, found the reports believable, giving Henry the success he needed. The exploration of the coast continued, and Henry continued to create maps and gather information about Africa.

Prince Henry died in 1460. He never gave Portugal great riches, but he did create more effective maps and navigational instruments. And, more importantly, he placed exploration in the mind of the public and the court.

Prince Henry may not have achieved all his goals, yet he effectively argued for their importance. The program he began in the early 15th century would change the nature of Portuguese power and commerce over the next 100 years.

montes della luna

cauo debona speransa

In the Wake of the Navigator

AFTER HENRY'S death, Portuguese exploration ceased for about nine years. Then, in 1469, Henry's nephew, King Alphonso V, found himself in financial trouble and decided to use exploration to get out of it. He made an agreement with Fernao Gomes, a wealthy trader from Lisbon. Gomes agreed to pay an annual fee to the crown, explore 100 leagues of coastline per year, and furnish the king with ivory from Africa at an inexpensive price. In exchange, Gomes would be the only person allowed to trade with the natives of Africa for five years.

Spurred by this financial impetus, the Gomes contract gave rise to a series of impressive discoveries. In five years,

Gomes explored a region from the southwest tip of Africa to just below the equator, covering more territory than Prince Henry had in more than 30 years.

By 1481, the five-year term of the contract was up, and the trading rights reverted back to the crown. Alphonso's son, John, was now King John II. In addition, trade from the African continent had finally become profitable, and Portugal received regular shipments of pepper, ivory, gold, and slaves. This valuable merchandise both increased the royal treasuries and the king's appetite for further exploration.

King John II sent a number of expeditions into the African interior and down its western coast. Some of the most important expeditions at this time were undertaken by Diogo Cão. Between 1480 and 1484, Cão explored the land below the equator and down the mouth of the Congo River.

These and other missions led to increasing interest in finding Prester John. In 1487, John II sent two missions in search of the mythical Christian: one by land, and one by sea. The land expedition, consisting of two men, followed a southeastern route across Africa. The sea mission

During Diogo Cão's voyages, the Portuguese began the practice of leaving stone crosses (called padrones) to mark their discoveries and as a testament of their Christian faith.

King John II

King John II (1455–1495) was viewed as a true Renaissance king. An active supporter of the arts and sciences, John II also achieved a variety of political goals. He maintained peace with Spain, decreased the power of the nobility, and signed a treaty setting the boundaries for Portuguese and Spanish exploration.

King John II will be remembered by history for his role in the Portuguese era of exploration. He continued the work of Henry the Navigator and set the stage for Vasco da Gama's first expedition, which was completed shortly after the king's death.

he trusted to Bartholomeu Dias, and it would become one of the most important voyages in the history of Portuguese exploration.

Bartholomeu Dias's expedition was carefully planned and featured some revolutionary practices. Dias was given two 50-ton caravels and a supply ship—a large ship that carried extra food and water for the voyage. This was the first Portuguese expedition ever to use a supply ship. The supply ship would allow the expedition to travel farther and remain on the open seas for a longer period of time. The king wanted this mission to succeed and would do everything in his power to make it happen.

The fleet set sail in August 1487. During the first leg of the mission, the Portuguese had favorable winds. The fleet passed Cape Bojador, once a fearsome barrier, without incident. One by one the fleet passed each marker of Portuguese exploration. By December, Dias and his ships were in unexplored territory.

On Christmas Day, they landed in Angra Pequena Bay

Bartholomeu Dias

Bartholomeu Dias was a prominent 15th-century navigator. Some historians believe he may have been a relative or descendant of João Dias, a famous Portuguese sailor. Others connect him to Diniz Dias, who discovered the Cape Verde Islands. Most historians feel these connections have yet to be clearly shown, however.

Dias was a member of the royal court and managed the royal warehouses. No one quite knows why King John II chose him to head the expedition to round the southern tip of Africa. Much is still unknown about Dias, but his place as a major figure in the story of Portuguese exploration remains secure. He died in 1500 on another mission to India.

to celebrate the holiday and rest for a bit. After this brief rest, they left their supply ship in this bay and continued sailing south. In early January, they encountered a powerful storm.

The *gale* raged for 13 days. Dias kept the fleet moving south and tried to maintain calm among the crew. The crew became frightened, however, giving themselves up for dead. Sea water leaked into the hull and the hold. Their stores of meat began to rot. Things did not look good.

Finally, the storm ended, and a gentle calm descended. On the first day after the storm, Dias headed east, hoping to reach the western coast of Africa. But after two days with no land in sight, he changed directions. He ordered the fleet north.

In less than a day, they sighted land. Dias's navigators believed that the storm had pushed them round the southern tip of Africa. To this day, no one is sure where Dias was when they sighted land. Most historians believe he was 200 miles east of the Cape of Good Hope, in the area of Mossel Bay.

Dias was not certain of their position. He wanted to be sure they had actually rounded the southern tip of Africa, so he kept the fleet headed north along the coast. After several days, he was sure. They had done it. They achieved what no Portuguese mariner had ever done—they had sailed around the southern tip of Africa.

Dias wanted to go further. He wanted to complete his mission, sailing into the Indian Ocean and on to India itself. His officers and crew had other ideas, however. They felt that simply rounding the southern tip of Africa was an achievement that would please the king. Furthermore, they feared their supplies would not last on such an arduous voyage.

Dias met with his captains. They refused to sail any farther, and insisted that the expedition return. Dias clearly was disappointed. He made them sign a document stating that this decision had been forced upon him. The document in hand, Dias ordered the fleet home.

The return voyage was a sad one for Dias. He felt that he had failed and was overcome with emotion when he saw the padrones that his men had left to mark their progress around the cape.

When they reached the supply ship, they found only three of the nine men they had left aboard still alive. The remaining men were very happy to see their comrades, whom they had feared would never return. Dias unloaded the supply ship and then ordered it **scuttled** and burned. The two caravels then headed back to Portugal, arriving in December 1488, more than 16 months after they had left.

The king's reaction to Dias's return remains somewhat

Bartholomeu Dias's men hoist a padrone into position to mark their landing site. Dias wanted to continue on around Africa into the Indian Ocean; however, most of his crew wanted to return to Portugal and he grudgingly agreed to turn back.

mysterious. He gave the cape a name (the Cape of Good Hope), which it retains to this day. Other than that, King John II seemed surprisingly unimpressed by Dias's expedition. Dias received no major awards, nor was a subsequent mission sent to follow up on Dias's discovery. This might have been because the king had problems at home, including an impending war with Spain.

Christopher Columbus's discovery of the Americas in 1492 further complicated things. Because it was believed that the Americas were close to the Azores, John II felt that these lands should rightly be the property of Portugal. Spain

When Dias returned to Portugal in 1488, an unknown sailor named Christopher Columbus was waiting in Lisbon's harbor. He had come to propose a plan to sail west, across the Atlantic, to reach the Indies. With the success of Dias's voyage east around Africa, however, King John was not interested. Columbus then took his plan to Portugal's rival, Spain, convincing the king and queen to support his journey in 1492.

had other ideas. Finally, the Pope negotiated an agreement, granting Spain the right to their new lands. This decision averted war and gave added impetus for further exploration. If Portugal could not have the lands in the west, they wanted to ensure their dominance of the sea route to Asia.

An expedition to follow up on Dias's expedition was in the planning stages when King John II died in 1495. But the new king, Manuel I, did not skip a beat. He followed up on John's plan and began to create a massive expedition to complete what Dias had begun.

Manuel's advisors argued against the massive expedition. They were afraid a large failure so early in his reign could hamper his ability to rule. In addition, they felt such an endeavor might worsen their already frayed relations with their neighbors. Manuel would not hear it. He understood the history of his nation and the role exploration had played in the last 100 years. He ordered the planning to start. King Manuel also chose a minor official and sailor named Vasco da Gama to head the expedition. It would prove to be an excellent choice.

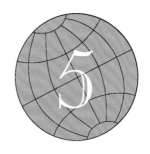

Vasco da Gama was a Portuguese nobleman who was chosen by the king to lead a mission to India in 1497. Gama was a strong, and at times ruthless, leader. His actions during the voyage also show him to have been smart and persistent.

Gama Sails for India

KING MANUEL I spared no expense on Vasco da Gama's expedition. He gave him four ships: the *San Gabriel*, the *San Rafael*, the *Berrio*, and a supply ship. On July 8, 1497, after religious ceremonies in a chapel built by Henry the Navigator, Vasco da Gama's fleet set sail for Africa. From there, they would sail on to India

The first leg of the expedition went well, but Gama's revolutionary attitude toward exploration was soon demonstrated. At the Cape Verde Islands, Gama made a surprising decision. Rather than hugging the African coast, as earlier explorers had done, he steered into open seas, making a wide loop and arriving near the southern tip of Africa on the third of November. For the next three days they hugged the coast, working their way slowly toward the Cape.

On November 7, they sailed toward land, finding low ground and a wide bay. Gama sent out a **launch**, searching for good anchoring grounds. The sailor in charge of the launch reported that the bay was clean and extended both east and west, providing excellent shelter from the wind. They named the bay Santa Helena.

The following day, they anchored in the bay and began cleaning and repairing their ships and exploring the lands and waterways around the bay. They discovered a river to the southeast and saw a variety of wildlife and several

"tawny-colored" natives dressed in animal skins.

On November 9, they captured one of these natives while he was gathering honey. Gama brought him aboard the ship, fed him at the commander's table, and dressed him in European clothing before setting him back ashore.

The next day, a group of 14 or 15 natives arrived at the bay, obviously interested in these curious visitors. Gama took advantage of their arrival to determine what riches lay in this land. He rowed ashore and showed the natives a variety of merchandise, including cinnamon, cloves, pearls, and gold. Gama's interaction with the natives continued well into the next day. By then he realized they had never

King Manuel I blesses Vasco da Gama before his expedition leaves Lisbon in July 1497. Manuel was only 21 years old when he took the throne in 1495. Although Gama's expedition had been planned under King John, Manuel continued his father's program of exploration. Manuel has been dubbed "the Fortunate" because he inherited this great program.

seen any of the merchandise he showed them. He gave them bells and tin rings and sent them on their way.

On November 12, an even larger group of natives arrived in the bay, perhaps as many as 50. Gama and his crew engaged in more **barter** with the natives, obtaining decorative jewelry and clothing.

During this encounter, Fernao Velloso asked Gama if he could follow the natives back to their village. After some discussion, Gama allowed Velloso to go.

Velloso followed the natives up the coast, watching as they caught a seal. They roasted the animal and offered it and some roots to the curious Velloso. Something must have occurred during the meal, however, because after it was finished, the natives told Velloso that he should return to his ship.

Velloso complied. Yet as he headed back toward the ships, some of the natives followed him, trying to remain hidden in the bush. When he reached the coast with the natives still in pursuit, Velloso grew frightened. He shouted to the ships for a launch to be sent.

Gama and others jumped in a boat to rescue the frightened Velloso. But before they could reach him, the natives attacked, injuring Velloso. This sudden outburst of violence confused Gama and his crew. Prior to the attack, the natives had seemed gentle and peaceful. Most historians agree that

Vasco da Gama

Vasco da Gama (1469–1524) was born in Sines, Portugal. As son of the town's governor, he was edu-cated as a nobleman and eventually served in the court of King John II. He also was a naval officer. In 1492, he successfully defended Portuguese colonies on the coast of Guinea from attacks by the French.

Gama's contemporaries viewed him as a ruthless man and a cruel taskmas-ter. In 1495, he was given command of an expedition to reach India by sea. Some historians claim the task had been given to his brother, Estavao, but that Estavao died before the mission began. Others claim the job was first offered to Gama's other brother, Paolo, who turned it down. This claim seems unlikely, since Paolo accompanied Gama on the expedition.

Velloso probably did something to anger them during the meal.

At dawn on November 16, after finishing their repairs and taking on wood, the fleet set sail. Astrolabe calcula-tions had them 96 miles from the Cape of Good Hope, but they could not be sure. None of the crew was familiar with that part of Africa.

They sailed south-southwest and reached the cape by Saturday. They tried to round the cape that night, but found it impassable. The following day, they tried again, but could not fight the strong south-southwest winds. Gama ordered the fleet out to sea to await more favorable winds. Finally, on Wednesday, November 22, with the wind at their backs, Gama's fleet succeeded in rounding the cape, arriving at Mossel Bay in present-day South Africa.

The fleet anchored for 13 days, taking on water and bartering with natives for cattle and sheep. Once again, however, their negotiation strategies seemed faulty, because the natives turned hostile. The crew returned to the ships, and Gama fired cannons at the natives. Thus, the sound of European cannon fire was heard for the first time in the Indian Ocean. The world was changing.

Over the next few months, Gama's fleet faced more problems. Each time they attempted to sail east, unfavorable winds would force them back to the coast. Unable to move east, they limped north, stopping many times to collect water and repair their ships.

On March 2, 1498, they landed in Mozambique. They found Muslims trading in precious metals, spices, and rare fabrics. From the traders, Gama's men learned many things about the region. However, they were forced to use their cannons again when a local *sheik* would not give them the water they needed.

On April 7, they anchored off the island of Mombassa, which is located off the coast of present-day Kenya. There, a pleasant *sultan* gave them sugarcane and citrus fruits. These eased the discomfort caused by *scurvy*, a disease that was common on long sea voyages.

As they continued north, Gama stopped in the port of Malindi. There he forced an Arab pilot named Ibn Majid to help him find his way to India. Majid was an experienced navigator and knew the Indian Ocean. With his help, Gama's fleet was finally able to cross the Indian Ocean and reach India on May 20, 1498.

It had been more than 100 years since the birth of Prince Henry the Navigator, but Portugal had finally completed its greatest mission. However, though it was a great success for the Portuguese to reach the strange eastern land, there were still problems ahead for Gama and his crew.

Senhor

posto queo capitam moor desta vossa frota e asy os
outros capitaães screpuam avossa alteza anoua do acha
mento desta vossa terra noua que se ora nesta naue
gaçam achou. nom leixarey tambem de dar disso
minha comta avossa alteza asy como eu milhor
poder ajmda que pera o bem contar e falar o saiba
pior que todos fazer. pero tome vossa alteza minha
jnoramçia por boa vontade. aqual bem certo crea q
que por afremosentar nem afear aja aquy de poer mais
ca aquilo que vy e me pareçeo. da marinhajem
e simgraduras do caminho nõ darey aquy cõ
ta avossa alteza por queo nom saberey fazer e os
pilotos deuem teer ese cuidado e por tanto Snor
do que ey de falar começo e diguo.
que apartida de belem como vossa alteza sabe foy segunda
feira ix de março. e sabado xiiij do dito mes amtre
as biij e ix oras nos achamos antre as canareas
mais perto da grã canarea e aly amdamos todo
aquele dia em calma avista delas obra de tres ou
quatro legoas. e domingo xxij do dito mes aas x
oras pouco mais ou menos ouuemos vista das jlhas
do cabo verde .s. dajlha de sã njcolaao segundo dito de pº
escolar piloto. e anoute segujmte aa segunda feira lhe
amanheceo se perdeo da frota vaasco datayde com
asua naao sem hy auer tempo forte nem contrairo
pera poder seer. fez o capitam suas deligençias pera
o achar a huũas e a outras partes e nom pareceo mais
e asy segujmos nosso caminho per este mar de lomgo
ata terça feira doitauas de pascoa que foram xxj
dias dabril que topamos alguũs synaaes de terra
seendo da dita jlha segundo os pilotos deziam obra de
bje lx ou lxx legoas. os quaaes herã mujta cam
tidade deruas compridas aque os mareantes
chamã botelho e asy outras aque tambem chamã
rrabo dasno. e aa quarta feira segujmte pola ma

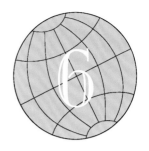

A letter from Pedro Álvares Cabral, a Portuguese sailor who followed Vasco da Gama's route to India. During his voyage, Cabral discovered the Brazilian coast of South America. Thanks to its sea route to Asia, tiny Portugal became one of Europe's richest and most powerful nations.

The Portuguese Empire

ON MAY 20, 1498, Gama and his crew sailed toward the coast of India, anchoring a few miles from the city of Calicut. Gama sent a representative ashore—a convict named Álvaro Vehlo. He encountered two Tunisians, who invited Vehlo to their lodgings and fed him bread and honey. After dining, the entire group returned to Gama's ship. Once on board, one of the Tunisians said in Portuguese, "A lucky venture, a lucky venture! Plenty of rubies, plenty of emeralds! You owe great thanks to God, for having brought you to a country holding such riches."

On May 28, 1498, Gama and 13 men set out to see the sultan, or ruler, of Calicut. On landing, they were met by a

This illustration from a 19th-century book shows Vasco da Gama and his men rowing ashore a few miles from the Indian city of Calicut. They had intended to anchor their ships closer, but one of Gama's pilots mistook another city for Calicut.

group of 200 armed men. They received Gama's men in a friendly manner, but the sight of their unsheathed swords frightened some of Gama's men.

The natives provided Gama with a palanquin (a type of closed litter carried by six men) and took him to a local lord to arrange his meeting with the sultan. When the arrangements were complete, they set off to the ruler's palace. They journeyed down a river crowded with boats, disembarked and followed a road crowded with people anxious to see the curious visitors.

Gama and his men were taken to a temple. This massive structure was built of stone with a giant brass column at its

entrance. The inside was deco-
rated with paintings and rows
of small brass bells. Gama and
his men prayed in the temple.

After leaving the temple,
they entered the main gates of
the city and were led to yet

> **Almost everything we know about Vasco da Gama's first voyage to India comes from the diaries of Álvaro Vehlo, a convict and member of Gama's crew.**

another temple. The crowds thickened as they exited the
temple, making movement through the streets almost
impossible. The sultan sent a local lord with several atten-
dants to escort Gama's men through the crowds. The escort
played loud music and fired guns as they led Gama's men
toward the palace.

The sun was setting as they entered the palace. They
passed through a large courtyard and four doors before
reaching the door to the sultan's chamber. They fought back

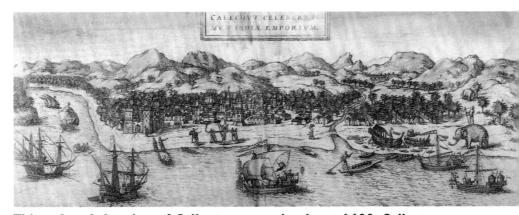

**This colored drawing of Calicut was made about 1600. Calicut was
an important port on the southwest of India.**

the crowds at each step. A small man greeted them at the door to the sultan's chamber. He embraced Gama and ushered him inside. The sultan lay on a large couch covered with green velvet and other fine fabrics.

Gama saluted the sultan in the Hindu manner, clasping his hands together, raising them over his head, then lowering them and quickly making fists. The sultan beckoned him forward. Gama did not move, knowing it was a breech of **protocol** to approach the sultan.

The sultan motioned for Gama's men to sit on a stone bench and had his servants bring water and fruit for them.

Vasco da Gama has an audience with the sultan of Calicut. Their 1498 meeting opened direct trade between Portugal and India, making Gama's country one of the richest in Europe.

The men enjoyed the fruit, especially a small fruit resembling a fig. This sight greatly pleased the sultan. Then the ruler told Gama to address his **courtiers**, suggesting they would confer all important information to him.

Gama told them that he was an ambassador from the king of Portugal and the message he held could only be delivered to another king. The sultan seemed to understand and suggested they move to an another room for privacy. Gama went into the small alcove that the ruler had indicated. Presently, the sultan joined him, flopping down on a couch and asking Gama what he wanted.

Gama told the sultan about the riches of Portugal and how his people had spent 60 years searching the land and seas for signs of Christian allies. He went on to explain that this was the purpose of their visit and that they did not seek gold or other riches. He also told the ruler of Calicut that the king of Portugal wished to be his friend and brother.

The sultan welcomed these kind words, telling Gama that he already considered the Portuguese king his brother. He promised to send ambassadors on Gama's return voyage. The two men spent much of the night talking about many things. Gama hoped this long conversation would help the Sultan trust him.

The following morning, Gama's men prepared a large group of presents for the sultan, including fabrics, hats, inexpensive jewelry, sugar, oil, and honey. Aware of local protocol, Gama informed the sultan's chain-of-command that he had presents for the king. However, when the sultan's men came to view the presents, they laughed and told Gama such gifts were not fit for a ruler. A present to the sultan must be gold, they informed him. Anything less, he would not accept.

Gama became upset. He told them that he did not bring gold, that he was an ambassador, not a merchant. These were his personal gifts, he said, and the best he could offer. If King Manuel ordered him to return, he would bring gold. Right now, however, he did not have it to give. He finished by stating that if the sultan did not want these gifts, he would put them back on the ship.

Gama was not allowed to see the sultan until the next day. The sultan was in a bad mood when Gama arrived. He had heard about the gifts, and felt Gama had lied to him. "You told me you came from a rich kingdom, but you brought me nothing. You told me that you had a letter for me, but I have not seen it," the sultan said.

> **Gama and his men mistook the Hindus of India for Christians due to the language barrier and the similarity between many Hindu and Catholic ceremonies.**

For the next two months, Gama tried to reassure the sultan. He was virtually held hostage as Muslim merchants attempted to loot the contents of his ship. Finally, shortly before he left, he was able to mend his relationship with the sultan, creating the beginnings of a more comfortable relationship. The sultan gave him the following letter to deliver to the King of Portugal. It read:

> Vasco da Gama, a nobleman of your house, came to me, and I received him gladly. In my land there is much cinnamon and much clove and ginger and pepper and many precious stones. What I want from your land is gold and silver and coral and scarlet cloth.

On August 29, 1498, Gama's fleet departed for Portugal. The return voyage was hard, as **monsoons** made crossing the Indian Ocean difficult. The crossing also affected the health of his crew, and Gama was forced to anchor in Malindi as they recovered. Unfortunately, the voyage home only brought more death and disease. When they finally sailed into Lisbon harbor in September 1499, it was with only two ships, the *Berrio* and the *San Gabriel*. Only 55 members of the original crew of 170 had survived the journey.

Despite the losses, Vasco da Gama's expedition was viewed as a huge success. Gama was awarded land and titles and was put in charge of several future expeditions. Most historians view Gama's accomplishment as the greatest of the age of exploration. While Columbus' discovery of the Americas may have had greater impact, Gama's journey

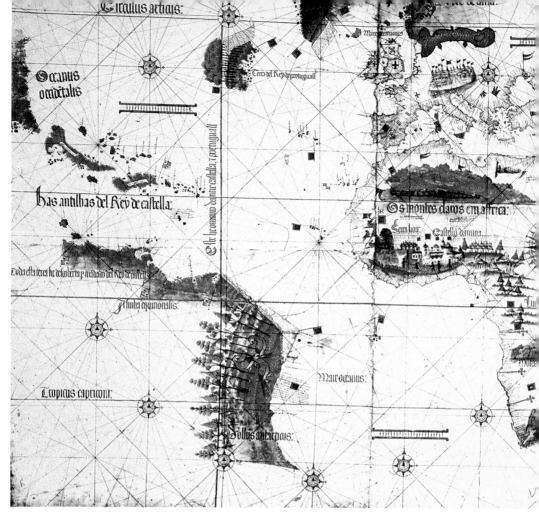

This Portuguese map of the world was made early in the 16th century, shortly after the voyages of Vasco da Gama and Pedro Cabral. Portuguese possessions are marked with red and blue flags, while Spanish discoveries are marked with the banner of Ferdinand and Isabella. At the lower left is Brazil, which Cabral discovered by

represented a greater *maritime* feat. Columbus found the Americas accidentally—he thought he was sailing to the Indies. Vasco da Gama, on the other hand, accomplished just what he set out to do—he sailed around the Cape of Good Hope to India, proving that sea travel to Asia was possible.

After Vasco da Gama's successful expedition, it seemed

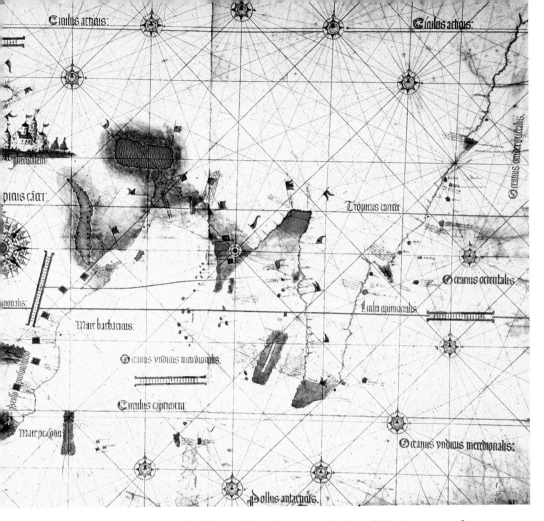

Circulus articus.

Circulus articus.

Circulus articus.

Oceanus amer criicalis.

Iherusalem.

piais cancr.

Tropicus cancri

Oceanus ocientalis

nooalis.

Linia equinoaalis

Mare barbancus.

Circulus yndicus mardionalis.

Oceanus yndicus meridionalis.

Circulus capricorni.

Mare persicon

Pollus antarticus.

accident in 1500. Maps also show a chain of Portuguese forts along the western coast of Africa, and settlements with which Portugal had established trade relationships in India and the east. The two flags in India represent Calicut and Goa, another city where Gama stopped to trade on his 1497–99 voyage.

that the creation of a Portuguese empire was the next logical step. In 1500, another fleet of Portuguese ships set sail for India. The commander was Pedro Álvares Cabral; one of the ship captains was Bartholomeu Dias. Cabral took a suggestion from Gama, and sailed far to the southwest, in an arc away from the coast of Africa. Cabral sailed so far that his men spotted land—the coast of South America, in present-day Brazil. Cabral claimed the land for Portugal and continued on his way around Africa.

Cabral's ships would make another important discovery on this voyage. While sailing north, a storm separated the Portuguese ships. The ship carrying Bartholomeu Dias sank during the gale. Another ship, captained by Lourenço Marques, landed on Madagascar, a large island off the coast of southeast Africa. Marques claimed this land for Portugal.

Cabral established trading posts at Calicut and another Indian city, Cochin, then returned to Portugal. His ships were filled valuable goods, as well as spices from the east: cloves, ginger, pepper, and cinnamon.

In 1502, Vasco da Gama sailed once again for India. This time he went not as an explorer, but as a conqueror. His mission was to make Calicut a Portuguese colony. In October, when he arrived on the coast of Calicut, he ordered the sultan to expel all Muslims from the city and surrender it to the Portuguese crown. The sultan tried to negotiate. Gama would have none of it.

He captured and hanged a number of Muslim traders and fishermen. He cut off their hands and feet and sent them to the sultan. The sultan quickly surrendered. Gama sailed home with his holds full of treasure, leaving five ships in command of the port. Gama returned home a hero.

With the capture of Calicut, one era had ended and

Vasco da Gama's caravels sink an Arab freighter in this illustration. Gama's ruthless tactics helped Portugal secure control of the Indies, and made his small country a world power.

another began. The Portuguese would use their seafaring skills to create a worldwide empire. Leaders such as Francisco de Almeida and Alfonso de Albuquerque established the small country's rule over the region. For nearly a century, the Portuguese would control trade between the Indies and Europe. After Portuguese sailors were blown off course and landed in Japan in 1557, Portugal would act as a middleman for trading between Japan and China.

Although Portugal's power declined by the end of the 16th century, the role it played in the age of exploration cannot be questioned. And it all began with a prince who dreamed of becoming a legend.

Chronology

1394 Prince Henry the Navigator is born.

1415 Prince Henry participates in the capture of Ceuta and is exposed for the first time to the riches of the African caravan trade.

1420 Captains under the command of Prince Henry discover the Madeira Islands.

1432 Portuguese sailors discover the Azores.

1434 Gil Eannes circumnavigates Cape Bojador.

1446 Portuguese sailors arrive at Cape Verde.

1460 Prince Henry the Navigator dies.

1469 King Alphonso V signs the Gomes contract, resulting in five years of unprecedented exploration.

1481 King John II ascends to the throne of Portugal.

1487 Bartholomeu Dias sets sail for the Cape of Good Hope.

1488 Dias rounds the Cape of Good Hope and returns to Portugal.

1492 Columbus discovers the Americas.

1495 King John II dies; Manuel I ascends to the throne.

1497 Vasco da Gama sails for India.

1498 On May 22, Vasco da Gama arrives in India.

1499 In September, Vasco da Gama returns to Portugal and receives a hero's welcome.

Chronology

1500 While sailing in a wide arc across the southwestern Atlantic to try to round Africa, the Portuguese sailor Pedro Álvares Cabral discovers Brazil. Also during this voyage, Lourenço Marques lands on Madagascar and claims it for Portugal. Bartholomeu Dias dies at sea;

1502 On his second mission to India, Vasco da Gama captures the Indian port of Calicut.

1524 Vasco da Gama dies on December 24.

1543 Portuguese traders blown off course became the first Europeans to land in Japan.

1572 Publication of Portugal's *Os Lusíadas*, by Luis Vaz de Camões, which begins with an account of Vasco de Gama's voyage to India and celebrates the heroes of Portugal's great age of exploration and expansion.

Glossary

armada—a fleet of warships.

astrolabe—an instrument used to observe and calculate the position of celestial bodies.

barter—to trade by exchanging one good or service for another.

caravel—a sturdy sailing ship developed by the Portuguese in the 15th century. A caravel had a broad hull, a high and narrow deck at the back, and usually three masts. Caravels were often rigged with both square and triangular, or lateen, sails.

cartographer—a person who makes maps.

circumnavigation—to go completely around, especially by water.

courtiers—people in attendance at a royal court.

cross-staff—an astronomical tool used to take measurements.

gale—a strong wind.

inlet—a bay in the shore of a sea, lake, or river.

latitude—one's relative position east or west on the earth.

launch—a large boat that operates from a ship.

league—a unit of distance, usually about three miles.

longitude—one's relative position north or south on the earth.

mariner—a person who navigates or assists in navigating a ship.

maritime—of, relating to, or bordering on the sea.

Glossary

monsoon—a period of heavy rainfall and high winds.

Muslim—a person who follows the Islamic religion.

navigable—deep enough and wide enough for ships to pass through.

protocol—the rules or conventions of correct behavior on official or ceremonial occasions.

scurvy—a disease caused by a deficiency of vitamin C. Symptoms include bleeding gums, loose teeth, aching joints, and internal bleeding. If untreated, it can lead to death. The disease was common on long voyages.

scuttle—to cut a hole through the bottom, deck, or side of a ship for the purposes of sinking it.

sheik—an Arab chief.

strait—a narrow passageway connecting two large bodies of water.

sultan—a king or ruler, especially of a Muslim state.

surge—a series of large waves.

Further Reading

Boorstin, D. J. *The Discoverers*. New York: Random House, 1983.

Cuyvers, Luc. *Into the Rising Sun: Vasco da Gama and the Search for the Sea Route to the East*. New York: TV Books, 1999.

Gallagher, Jim. *Vasco da Gama and the Portuguese Explorers*. Philadelphia: Chelsea House, 2000.

Hemming, J., ed. *Atlas of Exploration*. New York: Oxford University Press, 1997.

Moura, V. C. *Portugal and the Discoveries: The Meeting of Civilizations*. Seville: Commission of Portugal, 1992.

Russell-Wood, A. J. R. *A World on the Move: The Portuguese in Africa, Asia, and America 1415–1808*. New York: St. Martin's Press, 1993.

Internet Resources

The Portuguese Explorers

http://www.kn.pacbell.com/wired/fil/pages/listnewwormr.html

http://www.mariner.org/age/portexp.html

http://www.heritage.nf.ca/exploration/portuguese.html

Prince Henry the Navigator

http://www.mariner.org/age/princehenry.html

http://www.thornr.demon.co.uk/kchrist/phenry.html

Vasco da Gama

http://www.mariner.org/age/dagama.html

http://www.angelfire.com/ak/militaryorders/vascogama.html

Index

Africa, 7, 9, 13, 14, 16, 23–27, 29–35, 39–45

Alphonso V, king of Portugal, 29, 30

Americas, 35, 58

Asia, 7, 14, 36, 59

Atlantic Ocean, 13, 21

Azore Islands, 21, 36

Baldaya, Alphonso, 23–24

Berrio, 39, 58

Cadamosto, Alvise, 25

Calicut, 47–59

Cão, Diogo, 30

Cape Bojador, 21–23, 32

Cape of Good Hope, 33, 35, 40, 44, 58–59

Cape Verde, 25, 39

Christians, 14, 16, 30, 47, 51, 52

Columbus, Christopher, 35, 58

Dias, Bartholomeu, 7–11. 13. 31–36

Eannes, Gil, 22–25

Europe, 9, 14, 17, 18

Gama, Vasco da, 37, 39–45, 47–59

Gomes, Fernao, 29–30

Gomes, Diogo, 25, 26–27

Gonçalves, Antão, 25

Iberian Peninsula, 25

India, 8, 34, 39, 45, 47–58, 59

Islam (Muslims), 14, 16, 45, 52–59

John I, king of Portugal, 14

John II, king of Portugal, 30, 35, 36

Majid, Ibn, 45

Manuel I, king of Portugal, 36–37, 39, 51, 52, 53, 58

Middle East, 14

Pope Nicholas V, 26, 36

Portuguese exploration, 11, 13, 17–19, 21–27, 29–37, 45, 58, 59

Prestor John, 16, 26–27, 30

Prince Henry the Navigator, 14–19, 21–27, 29–30, 39, 45

San Gabriel, 39, 58

San Rafael, 39

St. Mary, 56

Tristão, Nuno, 25

Tunisians, 47

Vehlo, Ãlvaro, 47

Velloso, Fernao, 42–43

Photo Credits

About the Author

David Rutsala is a freelance writer who lives in Brooklyn, New York. This is his first book for Mason Crest.